Rosemary Hellyer-Jones
Peter Lampater

The Master Spies of Selby Road

Ernst Klett Verlag

Contents

Zu dieser Lektüre gibt es eine Compact-Cassette,
Klettnummer 571231

ISBN 3-12-571230-0

1. Auflage 1 5 4 | 1991 90

Alle Drucke dieser Auflage können im Unterricht nebeneinander benutzt werden, sie sind untereinander unverändert.
Die letzte Zahl bezeichnet das Jahr dieses Druckes.

Zeichnungen: Wolfgang Metzger, Mühlacker
Umschlagentwurf: Gebhardt, Korntal
Satz: Setzerei Lihs, Ludwigsburg
Druck: Stuttgarter Druckerei GmbH, Stuttgart
Printed in Germany

THE SELBY ROAD PEOPLE

Barbara Klein

Kevin and
Kate Pearson

Ronny Bennett

and his little
brother,
Timmy Bennett

1 Master Spy

"Bye-bye! See you tomorrow!" says Barbara.

She and Ronny and Kevin are going home from school. They are outside the Kleins' house now.

"Hey, wait," says Ronny. "Can't you come into my house for a few minutes? I want to show you something."

"O.K.," says Barbara.

"But what about homework?" says Kevin. "We've got a lot this time."

"There's still time for that after tea," says Ronny. "Come on!" So they all go into the Bennetts' house next door.

"What do you want to show us then?" asks Barbara on the way upstairs. "Has Timmy got a new potty or something?"

"Don't be silly! It's something really good," says Ronny, and he takes the other two into his room. He opens his cupboard and takes out a box.

"Master Spy*," reads Kevin. "Hey, that looks good. Is it a new game?"

"Not really," says Ronny. "It's a present from my aunt in London. Look in the box."

He opens it and takes a few things out. A false beard* and a grey wig* come out first.

"Disguises*!" he says.

"Let's try them on!" says Kevin.

master spy [mɑ:stə'spaɪ] Meisterspion
false beard [ˌfɔ:ls'bɪəd] falscher Bart
wig [wɪg] Perücke
disguise [dɪs'gaɪz] Verkleidung

"Wait. I must show you the other things first," says Ronny. "Look. This bottle has got invisible ink* in."

"Invisible ink?" says Barbara. "But I can see it! It isn't invisible at all."

"Oh, Barbara!" says Ronny. "The ink isn't invisible in the bottle! But when you write with it, it is. You can write secret messages* with it. Watch."

He gets a piece of paper and picks up a clean pen. Then he writes a few words with the invisible ink.

"See? It's invisible! Nobody can read it." Ronny gets a small candle* out of the box. "Now watch again."

He lights* the candle and holds the piece of paper over it. When the paper gets warm, the words in invisible ink start to go brown*.

invisible ink [ɪn'vɪzəbl'ɪŋk] unsichtbare Tinte
message ['mesɪdʒ] Nachricht, Botschaft
candle ['kændl] Kerze
to light [laɪt] anzünden
to go brown braun werden

"Hey, that's clever!" says Kevin. "Let me try!"

They all take turns, and have a good time. Just when Barbara is writing a silly message to Gordon Gossip, Mrs Bennett calls from downstairs.

"Ronny! Tea's ready!"

Kevin looks at his watch. "It's after five," he says. "I must go."

He and Barbara run downstairs.

"See you tomorrow!" Ronny calls after them. "Then we can try the disguises. And I can show you some secret codes*!"

code [kəʊd] Geheimschrift

2 Secret Messages

The next day, before* afternoon school, Kevin and Barbara ask Ronny about the codes.

"What about those secret codes?" asks Barbara.

"Can't you show us them now?" says Kevin. "We've still got five minutes."

"O.K. Well, we must start with an easy code," says Ronny. "Come over here." He takes an old exercise book out of his school-bag and finds a clean page. Then he writes something down.

"Well? Do you understand it?" he asks.

"Of course not," answers Barbara. "What does it mean?"

"Well, some letters don't mean anything," says Ronny. "Take away the first letter in every 'word'. Then look again."

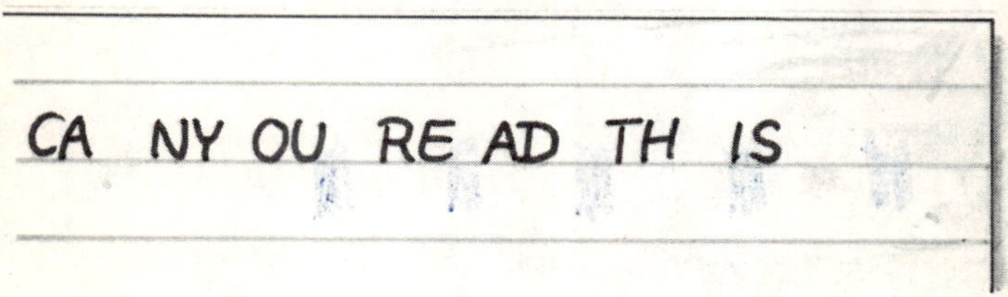

before [bɪ'fɔ:] vor

"It still doesn't mean anything!" says Kevin.

"Yes, it does!" says Barbara. "It says: CAN YOU READ THIS? – Yes, I can! Hey, Ronny, that's good! It's easy really."

"Codes are always easy when you know how they go," says Ronny. "Look, another code goes like this ..."

But it is time for afternoon school now. Mrs Griffin comes in, the children all go to their seats, and the English lesson* starts.

The lesson after English is German. In the middle of the lesson, when the children are writing an exercise, Kevin suddenly sees a small piece of paper on his desk*. It is from Barbara. He looks at it.

A minute later, the piece of paper is on the next desk – Ronny's desk! Ronny reads the message, then he writes an answer.

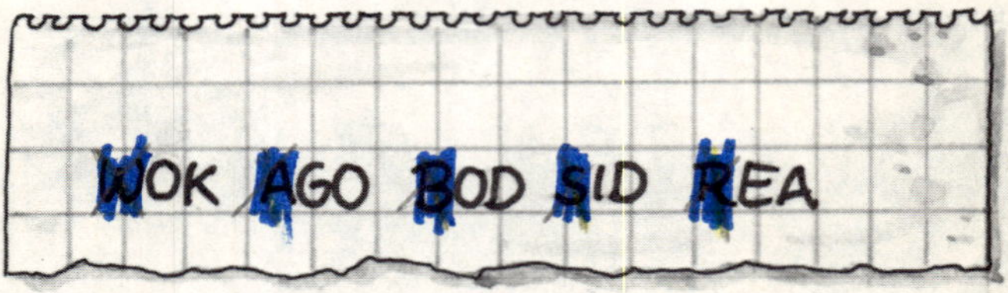

lesson ['lesən] Unterrichtsstunde
desk [desk] Schreibtisch, Pult

"Was machst du da, Ronny?" a voice says suddenly. It is Mr Drake, the German teacher. Ronny looks up.

"What? Er ... nothing, sir*," he says. "I mean – nichts!"

Everybody laughs. Mr Drake takes the piece of paper from Ronny and looks at it.

"Was ist denn das?" he asks.

"Das ist ein ... ein ... – Sorry, sir," says Ronny. "I don't know the word for it in German." Barbara tries not to laugh.

"Go on with the exercise, all of you!" says Mr Drake, and he throws Ronny's message away. "You, too, Barbara!"

On the way home after school, the three friends talk about Barbara's plan.

"Great idea!" says Kevin. "Half past five at Grosmont House, then. Perhaps Kate can come, too."

sir [sɜː] *höfliche Anrede einer männlichen Autoritätsperson*

3 Grosmont House

Grosmont House is a big old house in Old Farm Road, near Selby Road. Nobody lives there now, and the big garden round the empty house is very overgrown*. The children sometimes go there and play.

It is just after half past five when Barbara and Ronny climb over* the old garden wall. Kevin and Kate are waiting for them.

"Let's play sardines*," says Kate.

"Sardines?" says Barbara. "What's that?"

"Oh, don't you play that in Germany?" says Kate. "Well, one of us goes and hides*. Let's say I start. You others count* to fifty. Then you go and look for me. But you must all go different ways. Let's say Ronny finds me first. Well, he hides with me until someone else finds us. Then three of us hide together, and in the end the fourth person* finds us all – like sardines in a tin!"

"I see. That doesn't sound bad," says Barbara. "You hide first, Kate."

"Right!" says Kate. "Shut your eyes and count to fifty!"

Kate runs round the house. She has a good idea. She climbs up into an old apple-tree* and hides there. Soon the others are looking for her. They can't see her at all. But at

overgrown [əʊvə'grəʊn] überwuchert
over ['əʊvə] über
sardines [sɑ:'di:nz] Sardinen
to hide [haɪd] sich verstecken
to count [kaʊnt] zählen
person ['pɜ:sn] Person
tree [tri:] Baum

last Kevin looks up into the apple-tree and sees her. He waits until the others are gone, then he climbs up into the tree, too. A few minutes later, they see Barbara just under the tree. But she doesn't see them. Kevin starts to laugh.

"Ssh!" says Kate. But Barbara hears them. She looks up.

"Oh! There you are!" Soon she is up in the apple-tree, too.

"Let's hope this tree is strong," says Kevin. "You two girls are so heavy!"

"No, we're not!" says Barbara. "You are!"

"Quiet!" says Kate. "Ronny's coming!"

When Ronny finds them all, he wants to climb up, too.

"Don't!" says Kate. "Four of us is too much!"

"No, it isn't," says Ronny. He climbs up – and one of the branches* breaks. So he falls down very suddenly.

"Hey – are you O.K.?" calls Barbara.

"Of course I'm O.K!" shouts Ronny, and they all laugh.

Then suddenly they hear an angry voice.

"What's going on there? What are you children doing in that garden? Come out of there at once!"

"It's old Mrs Morton!" whispers* Ronny.

"You mustn't play in there! Don't you know that? It's private*."

"But nobody lives here," says Kate. "It's –"

"I tell you, it's private," the old lady calls from the road. "Come out, and don't let me see you in there again."

branch [brɑ:ntʃ] Ast
to whisper ['wɪspə] flüstern
private ['praɪvət] privat

4 SOS?

The four friends are on their way home.

"Why can't we play at Grosmont House?" says Kate. "We aren't doing anything wrong. Old Mrs Morton is silly."

"After all, it's not *her* house," says Barbara. "So *she* can't send us away."

"I don't know," says Ronny. "Perhaps it *is* private, really."

"Well, bye-bye, you two," says Kevin. "See you at school tomorrow."

* * *

Later that evening, when Kevin and Kate are getting ready for bed, Kate calls Kevin.

"Hey, Kevin! Come into the bathroom! Quick*!"

"What's the matter, Kate? What is it?"

"Come in here and have a look*."

Kevin goes into the bathroom and shuts the door. Kate is at the window. She is looking out into the night.

"Look over there," she says. "Do you see?"

Kevin goes to the window and looks out.

"Lights*!" he says. "Hey, that's funny. On – off – on – off. Those are signals*! Somebody's sending signals from a house over there."

quick [kwɪk] schnell
to have a look schauen
light [laɪt] Licht
signal ['sɪgnəl] Signal

"Perhaps it's Morse*," says Kate. "Yes, I'm sure it must be Morse. Perhaps it's an SOS*!"

"No, it's not that," says Kevin. "The SOS signal is different. But it's the Morse code, I'm sure."

"Where are the lights coming from?" asks Kate.

"From one of the big houses in that road behind the Bennetts' house," says Kevin. "Wait a bit. Isn't that – ?"

"Old Farm Road!" says Kate. "And those lights are coming from Grosmont House – that's it, I'm sure!"

Morse [mɔːs] Morse
SOS [esəʊˈes] SOS

5 Signals in the Night

The next day at school, Kevin tells Barbara and Ronny about the signals.

"Are you sure that you can see Grosmont House from your bathroom window?" asks Ronny.

"I think so," answers Kevin.

"Well, it's funny," says Barbara. "Grosmont House is empty, we know that. Or does somebody live there after all?"

"No," says Ronny. "The house is empty. But perhaps somebody goes there at night and sends signals from a window upstairs."

"But why?" says Barbara. "And who are the signals for? What do they mean?"

"Hey! I've got an idea!" says Ronny. "You know that Master Spy box? Well, I think the Morse code is in there. Let's try to learn it."

"Oh yes! Then, if* we see the signals again, perhaps we can understand them," says Kevin. "If it really is Morse."

"Well, we must watch for* them every night," says Barbara. "We can take turns."

"O.K.," says Ronny. "I can watch for them tonight* from my bedroom window. I can see Grosmont House from there. If I see the lights, I can telephone you."

if falls, wenn
to watch for s.th. Ausschau halten nach etwas
tonight [tə'naɪt] heute abend

"Fine," says Kevin.

"But if it's late, and we're in bed?" says Barbara. "We can't go to the telephone then."

"I know what," says Ronny. "When I ring up, I can put the receiver* down after the second ring*. That can be my signal to you. If that happens, it means I can see the lights. O.K?"

* * *

It is ten past nine. Kate is reading in bed. Suddenly the telephone rings. Kate sits up in bed and listens. One ring. Two rings. No more. It must be Ronny! She gets out of bed, rushes to the door and runs to the bathroom. On the way she nearly runs into Kevin. They laugh, go into the bathroom together, and shut the door with a bang.

"What's going on there?" Mrs Pearson calls from the sitting-room. "Go to bed, you two!"

But Kate and Kevin are still in the bathroom. They are looking out of the window.

"Yes, look! Those lights again!" says Kevin. "What can it all mean?"

"Perhaps Ronny has an idea," says Kate. "He's got the code. We must ask him about it tomorrow."

receiver [rɪ'si:və] Hörer
ring klingeln, läuten

6 The Mystery of the Empty House

Barbara is on her way to school. But she is walking a different way today. She is going down Old Farm Road. She looks at her watch. Ten to nine. "Oh dear, I'm a bit late," she thinks. "I must rush*!"

But when she gets to Grosmont House, she stops. There is a car outside, and a man with a briefcase* in his hand is walking up to the house. Barbara is surprised. Who can the man be? What is he doing at the empty house? There is no time to find out. She looks at the number of the car – YUG 616 W – and runs down the road towards Fulford School.

* * *

"Well, it's a mystery*," says Ronny.

"The Mystery of the Empty House," says Kevin. "First old Mrs Morton tells us not to play at Grosmont House. Then we see lights there at night. And now Barbara sees a man there."

"Hey, Ronny! What about those signals? *Are* they Morse?" asks Barbara.

"I don't think so," says Ronny. "But I'm not sure. I don't really know the code yet, and it's not easy to follow* the signals and look at the code in my little book at the same time."

to rush [rʌʃ] eilen
briefcase ['bri:fkeɪs] Aktentasche
mystery ['mɪstərɪ] Geheimnis, Rätsel
to follow ['fɒləʊ] folgen

"Well, we really *must* find out what's going on," says Barbara. "Perhaps we can go there after tea again."

"No, let's go tonight," says Ronny.

"Tonight? When it's dark?" says Kevin. "Are you sure that's a good idea?"

"Well, we know that someone goes there at night and sends those signals. So, if we want to know more about it, we must go then, too."

"Right," says Barbara. "Hey, Ronny! Let's put on those disguises! You know, the false beard and the wig and everything!"

Kate laughs. "Oh yes! Great idea!"

"Well, O.K., but I'm the Master Spy, remember," says Ronny.

* * *

It is Friday evening. There is no school on Saturday, so the friends can stay out late. Just right for their plans! At quarter to nine, four strange* people come out of the Bennetts' house.

"Stay behind me, everybody!" calls Ronny. "And remember to be quiet when we get to Grosmont House."

"O.K., boss*!" laughs Barbara.

"Hey, wait for me," cries Kate. "I can't see the way through these silly glasses*!"

"Take them off then," says Kevin.

"But they're my disguise!"

strange [streɪndʒ] seltsam, ungewöhnlich
boss [bɒs] Chef
glasses ['glɑ:sɪz] Brille

"Fine disguise," answers Kevin. "Everybody can see it's you when you're wearing them – but *you* can't see anything at all!"

"Quiet, you two," says Ronny. "We're nearly there now. Ssh!"

7 The Room Upstairs

"Where can we get in?" whispers* Kate.

"Well, we can't go in through the front door," says Barbara. "That's locked."

"Perhaps there's a window open," whispers Kevin. "Let's look round."

The four friends walk round the house. Everything is very quiet. It is dark, so they switch on* their torches*. At the back of the house, Ronny stops.

"Hey, look at this!" he whispers. "A broken* window – what luck!"

He puts his hand through the broken window and opens it. He climbs in and the others follow.

"Now where do we go?" asks Kevin.

"Upstairs, of course," says Kate. "That's where the signals always come from."

"Don't make a noise, now!" whispers Ronny when they go through the hall. "Be extra careful on the stairs."

At the top of the stairs they look round.

"Look, that door's open," whispers Kevin. "Perhaps that's the room where the signals come from."

"Let's go in and have a look," says Barbara.

They go into the room and shut the door. In the light of their torches they see that the room is empty. There are a few old empty boxes on the floor. Nothing else.

to whisper ['wɪspə] flüstern
to switch on [swɪtʃ] einschalten
torch [tɔ:tʃ] Taschenlampe
broken ['brəʊkən] zerbrochen, kaputt

"Hey, look!" Kate calls from the window. "I think this must be the room where the signals come from. I can see the back of the Bennetts' house from here. That is, I *think* it's the Bennetts'."

"Let *me* have a look!" says Ronny. He rushes to the window, but doesn't look where he is going. He falls over a box. Bang! What a noise!

"Hey, be quiet, Ronny!" says Kate. "*Must* you make so much noise?"

"O.K., O.K," says Ronny. "I –"

"Ssh! Listen!" whispers Barbara suddenly. "What's that?"

There is a noise – on the stairs. Is it on the stairs? Is somebody coming upstairs?

"Switch the torches off and hide behind the door!" whispers Kate. "Quick!"

They do what Kate says. Everything is quiet, then they hear another noise. A noise at the door! Is somebody coming in? No, nobody is opening the door. It is a different noise. Very different. Soon they all know what it is. Someone is locking* the door!

to lock zuschließen

8 Prisoners

For a minute or two, they are all too afraid to speak. They hear more noises. Somebody is going down the stairs now. The next noise comes from the garden. Somebody – two people, or is it only one? – is running through the garden, and out into the road.

Kevin tries to open the door. But it is locked, of course.

"Now what do we do?" he says.

"What about the window?" says Barbara. "Let's try that."

They can open the window, but they can't get out that way, it is much too high. Kate looks out.

"Can't we climb out of here and get on a branch of that big apple-tree?"

"Don't be silly, Kate," says Ronny. "That tree's too far away. You can see that."

"Well, what *can* we do, then?" asks Kate. "Can't *you* think of anything? You're the Master Spy."

"Be quiet, Kate!" Ronny sounds angry now.

"No!" says Kate. "This is all *your* fault*, Ronny. First you say *we* must all be quiet. And then *you* make all the noise!"

"And when Kate has a good idea," says Barbara, "you say she's silly. I think *you're* silly."

"No, I'm not!" shouts Ronny. "And it isn't my fault! It's that stupid* box!" He kicks it into the corner.

"Oh, be quiet, you three," says Kevin, and sits down on an empty box. "Let's try to think."

fault [fɔ:lt] Schuld
stupid ['stju:pɪd] dumm, blöd

"The fact* is, we're prisoners*," says Barbara. "Secret codes and invisible ink and disguises all sound exciting, but they can't help us a bit now. We aren't really spies at all."

* * *

"I've got an idea," says Kate at last. "Let's open the window and shout for help."

"But the other houses are too far away. Nobody can hear our voices from here," says Barbara.

"Be quiet a minute!" whispers Ronny. "I think I can hear someone downstairs again. Ssh!"

They all listen. Yes, something is going on in the hall. Somebody is down there.

"Switch all the torches off!" whispers Kate. "They're coming back!"

"Oh no!" whispers Kevin. "What can we do now?"

Nobody answers. They are all afraid now. The little room is dark and cold. They stand together in a corner and listen. They can hear footsteps* on the stairs now. A lot of footsteps this time. How many people are coming up? Three? Four? Suddenly there is a noise at the door. Someone opens it, and Barbara screams.

"What's all this, then? What's going on here?" says a man's voice. The light of a big torch shines on the children. "Well, I never*! – Come in here and have a look, you two!

fact [fækt] Tatsache
prisoner ['prɪznə] Gefangener
footsteps ['fʊtsteps] Schritte
to scream [skri:m] schreien
Well, I never! [ˌwelaɪ'nevə] Nein, so was!

Burglars, you say? Squatters*? Why, it's only a bunch of kids*! In disguise, too!"

"What are all you kids doing here?" asks another voice. An angry voice this time.

"The police!!" cries Kevin. "But who – ?"

Behind the two policemen*, at the open door, they can now see two faces. Boys' faces.

"David Fletcher!" cries Ronny.

"Peter Wilson!" says Kate. "What are you two doing here?"

"That's just what we want to ask *you*!" says David. "What are you doing in our den*?"

squatter ['skwɒtə] Hausbesetzer
a bunch of kids [ˌbʌntʃəv'kɪdz] ein paar Kinder
policeman [pə'li:smən] Polizist
den [den] Versteck, Bude

"Your den?!" says Barbara. "But –"

"Our *private* den!" says Peter. "We often come here in the evenings and send signals to Ben and Mandy."

"We've got a secret code," says David.

"Oh no!!" says Ronny.

"Well, then, what are *you* all doing here? And why have you got those funny disguises on?" asks Peter. "Come on. Tell us."

Ronny and the others explain* everything.

"Well, you really *are* master spies, all of you," says the first policeman. But the other policeman looks angry.

"You kids* are wasting* our time," he says. "Don't you know that? We've got lots of other jobs to do!"

"Sorry we aren't burglars or squatters," says Barbara. "Sorry we're wasting your time like this. We –"

"Never mind about that!" laughs the first policeman. "Come on, Fred, don't be too angry with them, now. They're a nice bunch of kids."

"Hm. Well, they can't play here, you know that, Tom. Workmen* are going to* be here next week."

"Workmen?" says Kate. "But why?"

"They're going to pull this house down*," the second policeman explains. "The City Council* wants to build* some new flats here."

"New flats? Oh, so that explains the man with the brief-case here this morning," says Barbara.

to explain [ɪk'spleɪn] erklären
kid Kind
to waste [weɪst] verschwenden, vergeuden
workman ['wɜ:kmən] Arbeiter, Handarbeiter
They are going to Sie werden, sie haben es vor
to pull down abreißen
City Council [ˌsɪtɪ'kaʊnsəl] Stadtverwaltung
to build [bɪld] bauen

"You mean Mr Long from the City Council?" says the first policeman. "Well, never mind. I tell you what. You can all play up here until the workmen arrive. I think there's even an attic at the top of the house. You can look through all the old things up there if you like. Nobody wants them any more. Who knows what you master spies can find?"

"Hm," says the other policeman again, and looks at Ronny and his friends. "Well, out of here now, all of you! And don't come in here at night again, do you hear?"

9 The Attic

"Wait!" cries Timmy, "Wait for me!"

"O.K., Timmy," calls Ronny. "I'm waiting."

It is Saturday morning. The four friends are on their way up to the attic at Grosmont House. David and Peter are not with them. But Timmy is there. Ronny picks him up and carries him up the stairs.

"Come on, Ronny!" shouts Kate. "We're in the attic! Come and have a look at all the things!"

Soon they are all up there together. There are a lot of old things in the attic. Old boxes, and a big old cupboard. A broken bike, a table, and a funny old chair with a broken leg. Everything is very dirty.

"Let's open the boxes," says Barbara. "Perhaps there's something interesting inside*."

They open three big boxes. There are some old magazines in one box – but there is nothing at all in the other two.

"What about this box over here?" says Ronny. "It's very heavy. Let's see what's inside."

But the box is locked, and there is no key.

"Let's take it to my house," says Ronny. "We can try to open it with Dad's tools*."

"O.K.," says Kevin. "I think we can carry it."

"Where's Timmy?" asks Kate when they are on the stairs with the box.

inside [ɪn'saɪd] darin
tools [tu:lz] Werkzeug

Ronny goes back. Timmy is behind the big cupboard. He is looking at something. An old rocking-horse*.

"Come on, Timmy. Time to go home now. Leave that old thing."

"No, Ronny. I want it. Please!"

"What? This dirty old rocking-horse? But it looks terrible!"

"No, it doesn't," says Timmy. "I like it."

"Well, O.K., then," says Ronny. "But don't be surprised if Mum throws it away."

* * *

Half an hour later, they are all in the Bennetts' sitting-room. Ronny's parents are out. Timmy is riding on the old rocking-horse in one corner, and Kate is looking after him. In another corner, Ronny, Barbara and Kevin are trying to open the heavy box. They have got Mr Bennett's tools, but they still can't open it.

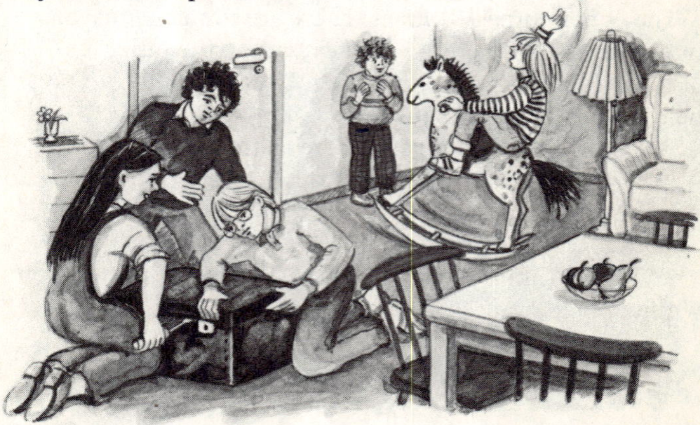

rocking-horse ['rɒkɪŋˌhɔːs] Schaukelpferd

"We must break the lid, then," says Ronny.

"O.K. That's the best way," says Barbara. "Let me try."

"Hey, you three." shouts Kate. "Watch me on Timmy's rocking-horse! Look how high I can go!"

But the others don't look up. The box is much too interesting. At last the lid comes off, and they look inside. But they don't find anything exciting – only old books and papers. How disappointing*!

Suddenly, just when they are putting everything back in the box, there is a terrible noise from the other corner of the room. Bang!

"Help!"

"Oh, Kate!" cries Timmy's small voice.

At last the other three look up. They see Kate on the floor, and the rocking-horse on its side*. And they see the Bennetts' new reading-lamp* on the floor, too – broken.

disappointing [ˌdɪsəˈpɔɪntɪŋ] enttäuschend
side [saɪd] Seite
reading-lamp [ˈriːdɪŋˌlæmp] Leselampe

10 The Rocking-Horse

"Typical!" shouts Kevin. "Kate, you're terrible!"

"Sorry!" says Kate. "Sorry, Ronny."

"Oh, Kate!" says Ronny. "That lamp is new."

For a minute or two, nobody says anything. How are they going to tell Ronny's parents? The lamp looks expensive*.

"That stupid rocking-horse!" shouts Ronny at last, and he kicks it. He is angry now. He kicks the rocking-horse again. And again.

"Don't!" says Timmy. "Don't, Ronny!"

But Ronny is really angry now, and he kicks it again. This time, it is too much for the old horse. Its side bursts*, and the stuffing* comes out. Timmy starts to cry. The rocking-horse looks terrible now.

"Don't cry, Timmy," says Barbara. "Perhaps we can repair it."

She picks the horse up again, and tries to put the stuffing back. But when she puts her hand in the hole, she feels something strange inside. Something cold.

"Hey – what's this?" She pulls something out, and looks at it. "Look at this! An old coin*!"

"Let me see!" shouts Kevin. "Hey – it looks like gold!"

"Treasure!" cries Kate, and she pulls more stuffing out.

expensive [ɪk'spensɪv] teuer
to burst [bɜ:st] aufplatzen
stuffing ['stʌfɪŋ] Füllung
coin [kɔɪn] Münze

Another coin falls on the floor. “Treasure!”
“Can't be,” says Ronny.
“Must be!” says Kate.

*   *   *

“These are the coins,” says Mr Bennett. “Well, Mr Brown, the question is – how much are they worth*?”

Ronny, Barbara, Kevin and Kate are with Mr Bennett. They are at Brown's antique shop* in Petergate. Mr Brown looks at the coins, then he goes to the back of the shop and fetches a big black book.

“Just a minute, Mr Bennett,” he says. “I can soon tell you. They're sovereigns*, of course. But –”

“Sovereigns?” shouts Ronny. “So they really *are* gold coins!”

“Treasure!” says Kate. “Treasure!!” She likes the word “treasure” – it sounds so exciting.

“Well, just a minute,” says Mr Brown again, and opens the big book. “Let me see, now. This is the page. Ah yes!” He puts his finger on the page. “Well now, you're very lucky people. Very lucky! These sovereigns are worth about £50 each*.”

“£50 each?” cries Ronny. “That much?!”

“And there are nine coins,” says Kevin. “So that means they're worth –”

“£450!” shouts Kate.

“But is it really our money*?” asks Barbara. “Grosmont

to be worth [wɜ:θ] wert sein
antique shop [æn'ti:kʃɒp] Antiquitätenladen
sovereign ['sɒvrɪn] alte britische Goldmünze
each [i:tʃ] je, pro Stück
money ['mʌnɪ] Geld

House belongs to* the City Council now. So don't the coins belong to the Council, too?"

"Not really," says Mr Bennett. "Gold sovereigns like this are treasure. And when people find treasure, it nearly always goes to museums. Of course, these are only a few coins, and Mr Long from the City Council tells me the Museum doesn't want them. They've got enough* old coins like these. So you can have them, he says – that's O.K."

"But that's great!" shouts Ronny.

"What are we going to do with the money?" asks Kevin.

"Let's have a day out together," says Barbara. "Perhaps we can go to Scarborough*."

"But first we must buy a new lamp for the Bennetts' sitting-room," says Kate. "And I know another thing! We can buy Timmy a lovely new rocking-horse."

"Great idea!" says Ronny. "A present from the four Master Spies of Selby Road!"

to belong to [bɪˈlɒŋ] gehören
enough [ɪˈnʌf] genug
Scarborough [ˈskɑːbrə] berühmtes Seebad in der Nähe von Whitby